A SIMPLE FAMILY BREVIARY
for Home, School, or Work

**from the Psalms of Saint Francis of Assisi
and the Commons of Mary and the Saints**

**simple once-daily prayer
suitable for a family, the classroom,
midday at work, and with co-workers**

idjc press

idjc.org

A Simple Family Breviary
for Home, School, or Work
from the Psalms of Saint Francis of Assisi
and the Commons of Mary and the Saints
copyright © 2012
Stephen Joseph Wolf

For more information about the Psalms of Saint Francis of Assisi see
The Geste of the Great King by Laurent Gallant, OFM and Andre Cirino, OFM,
© 2001 The Franciscan Institute, Saint Bonaventure University, New York.

Songs from the public domain appeared previously in *Hinge Hour Singer*.
The Commons Psalms are drawn from *Best of the Psalter*.

Illustrations are by Angie Bosio.

Published by idjc press and distributed by Ingram Books.
Contact steve@idjc.info.   **Visit idjc.org**

ISBN 978-1-937081-02-7

Large print and e-book editions are available.
idjc press books are available from
St. Mary's Bookstore in Nashville and fine bookstores everywhere.

PREPARATION

A. Check the calendar of saints (pages 4-8)
   to see if a "commons psalm" is suitable.
B. If desired, choose a passage of scripture.

AN ORDER FOR PRAYER

1. Song of the season or month
2. Psalm of the season or month
3. Psalm of the day of the week
4. Scripture passage or an "Our Father"
5. Closing praises (page 102)

A SIMPLE FAMILY BREVIARY

A Calendar Of Saints

including solemnities, feasts, and memorials

JANUARY

 1 **Solemnity: Mary, the Mother of God**   Luke 2:16-21
 2 Basil the Great, 379, & Gregory Nazianzen, 389, bishops & doctors
 3 Holy Name of Jesus
 4 Elizabeth Ann Seton, 1821, widow & founder of Sisters of Charity
 5 John Neumann, 1860, bishop of Philadelphia
 6 Blessed Andre Bessette of Montreal, 1937, worker & religious
13 Hilary, 368, bishop of Poitiers & doctor
17 Anthony of Egypt, 356, hermit & abbot
20 Sebastian of Rome, 288(?), martyr
21 Agnes, beginning of 4th century, at age 12, virgin & martyr
22 Day of Prayer for the Legal Protection of the Unborn (USA)
23 Vincent of Valencia in Spain, early 4th C., deacon & martyr
24 Frances de Sales, 1622, bishop of Geneva & doctor
25 **Feast: Conversion of Paul, Apostle**   Mark 16:15-18
26 **Timothy & Titus, bishops**   Luke 10:1-9
28 Thomas Aquinas, OP, 1274, priest & doctor
31 John Bosco, 1888, inspired founding of Salesians, priest & teacher

FEBRUARY

 2 **Feast: Presentation of the Lord**   Luke 2:22-40
 3 Blaise, early 4th century, bishop of Sebaste in Armenia & martyr
 5 Agatha of Sicily, mid 3rd century, virgin & martyr
 6 Paul Miki, SJ, and Companions, 1597, all martyrs of Nagasaki
10 Scholastica of Nursia, 543, virgin
11 Our Lady of Lourdes, apparition to St. Bernadette in 1858
14 Cyril, 869, and Methodius, 885, monks & bishops
17 Seven Founders of the Order of Servites, mid 13th C in Florence
21 Peter Damian, 1072, bishop of Ostia & doctor
22 **Feast: Chair of Peter, Apostle**   Matthew 16:13-19
23 Polycarp, 155, bishop of Smyrna & martyr burned at the stake

MARCH

 3 Katherine Drexel, 1955, virgin & founder Missionary Sisters
 7 Perpetua and Felicity of Carthage, 203, martyrs
 8 John of God, 1550, founder in Spain of Order of Hospitallers
17 Patrick of Ireland, 461, bishop of Armagh
18 Cyril of Jerusalem, 386, bishop of Jerusalem & doctor
19 **Solemnity: Joseph, Husband of Mary**   Matthew 1:16-24a
25 **Solemnity: The Annunciation of the Lord**   Luke 1:26-38

APRIL

4 Isidore, bishop of Seville & doctor

7 John Baptist de La Salle, 1719, founder of the Christian Brothers

11 Stanislaus, 1079, bishop of Cracow & martyr

21 Anselm, 1109, bishop of Canterbury & doctor

25 **Feast: Mark, Evangelist** Mark 16:15-20

29 Catherine of Siena, O.P. 3rd Order, 1380, virgin & doctor

MAY

1 **Joseph the Worker, carpenter** Matthew 13:54-58

2 Athanasius, 373, bishop of Alexandria & doctor

3 **Feast: Philip and James, Apostles** John 14:6-14

10 Damian de Veuster of Moloka'i, Hawaii, 1889, leper & priest

13 Our Lady of Fatima

14 **Feast: Matthias, Apostle** John 15:9-17

15 Isidore of Madrid, 1130, farmer

21 Christopher Magallanes & 24 Companions, 1915-37, martyrs

25 Venerable Bede, 735, Benedictine priest & doctor

26 Philip Neri, 1595, priest & founder of the Oratorians

31 **Feast: Visitation of Mary and Elizabeth** Luke 1:39-56

JUNE

1 Justin of Samaria & Rome, 165, martyr

3 Charles Lwanga of Uganda and 21 Companions, 1885-87, martyrs

5 Boniface of Germany, 754, Benedictine abbot, bishop & martyr

11 **Barnabas, apostle** Matthew 10:7-13

13 Anthony of Padua, OFM, 1231, priest & doctor

21 Aloysius Gonzaga, 1591, age 23, Jesuit scholastic

22 John Fisher and Thomas More of England, 1535, martyrs

24 **Solemnity: Birth of John the Baptist** Vigil: Luke 1:5-17

Day: Luke 1:57-66,80

28 Irenaeus of Lyons, 202, bishop & martyr

29 **Solemnity: Peter and Paul, Apostles** Vigil: John 21:15-19

Day: Matthew 16:13-19

30 First Martyrs of Rome, 64

Knowledge of ourselves is the necessary and only step
by which we can ascend to the knowledge and love of God.
St. Anthony, January 17

In your nature, O eternal Godhead, I shall know my own nature.
St. Catherine of Siena, April 29

JULY

1 Blessed Junipero Serra of California, 1784, Franciscan priest
3 **Feast: Thomas, Apostle** John 20:24-29
4 Independence Day (USA)
5 Elizabeth of Portugal, 1336, 3rd Order Franciscan, queen & widow
6 Maria Goretti of Corinaldi, 1902, age 12, virgin & martyr
11 Benedict of Nursia, 547, abbot & founder of the Benedictines
13 Henry II, 1024, emperor & husband to St. Cunegund
14 Blessed Kateri Tekakwitha of the Mohawks, 1680, virgin
15 Bonaventure, OFM, 1274, bishop of Albano & doctor
16 Our Lady of Mount Carmel, 12th century hermits
18 Camillus de Lellis, 1614, priest & founder of Clerks Regular (MI)
22 **Mary Magdalene** John 20:1-2,11-18
25 **Feast: James, Apostle** Matthew 20:20-28
26 Joachim and Ann, parents of Mary, grandparents of Jesus
29 **Martha** John 11:19-27
30 Peter Chrysologus, mid 5th century, bishop of Ravenna & doctor
31 Ignatius of Loyola, 1556, priest & founder of the Society of Jesus

AUGUST

1 Alphonsus Liguori, 1787, founder: Redemptorists, bishop & doctor
4 John Mary Vianney of Ars, 1859, patron of parish priests
6 **Feast: Transfiguration**
      A Matthew 17:1-9   **B** Mark 9:2-10   **C** Luke 9:28b-36
8 Dominic, 1221, priest & founder: Order of Preachers (Dominicans)
9 Teresa Benedicta (Edith Stein), 1942 at Auschwitz, Carmelite,
                                virgin & martyr
10 **Feast: Lawrence, 258, Deacon & Martyr** John 12:24-26
11 Clare of Assisi, 1253, virgin & founder of the Poor Clares
14 Maximilian Kolbe, OFM Conv, 1941 at Auschwitz, priest & martyr
15 **Solemnity: Assumption of Mary** Vigil: Luke 11:27-28
                                Day: Luke 1:39-56
20 Bernard, 1153, Cistercian abbot of Clairvaux & doctor
21 Pius X, 1914, pope
22 Queenship of Mary
23 Rose of Lima, Peru, 1617, age 31, 3rd Order Dominican & virgin
24 **Feast: Bartholomew, Apostle** John 1:45-51
27 Monica of Tagaste in Africa, 387 in Ostia, mother of Augustine
28 Augustine, 430, bishop of Hippo in Africa & doctor
29 **Passion of John the Baptist** Mark 6:17-29

SEPTEMBER

 3 Gregory the Great, 604, monk, pope & doctor
 8 **Feast: Birth of Mary**   Matthew 1:1-16,18-23
 9 Peter Claver, SJ, 1654, priest & missionary to Columbia
13 John Chrysostom, 407, bishop of Constantinople & doctor
14 **Feast: The Exaltation of the Holy Cross**   John 3:13-17
15 Our Lady of Sorrows   Luke 2:33-35
16 Cornelius, 253, pope & martyr,
    & Cyprian, 258, bishop of Carthage & martyr
20 Andrew Kim Taegon, 1847, priest,
    & the 102 Companions, martyrs in Korea
21 **Feast: Matthew, Apostle & Evangelist**   Matthew 9:9-13
23 Pius (Padre Pio) of Pietrelcina, 1968, Capuchin priest
26 Cosmas and Damian, 303, physicians & martyrs
27 Vincent de Paul,1660, priest & founder:
      Vincentians & Daughters of Charity
29 **Feast: Michael, Gabriel, & Raphael, archangels**   John 1:47-51
30 Jerome of Bethlehem, 420, priest & doctor

OCTOBER

 1 Therese of the Child Jesus, 1897, Carmelite of Lisieux, virgin & doctor
 2 Guardian Angels   Matthew 18:1-5,10
 4 Francis of Assisi, 1221, founder of the Order of the Franciscans
 6 Blessed Marie-Rose Durocher, 1849, virgin & founder: Sisters of the Holy Name
 7 Our Lady of the Rosary
11 Blessed John XXIII, anniversary of 1962 opening of Vatican II
15 Teresa of Avila, 1582, Carmelite, virgin & doctor
16 Margaret Mary Alacoque, 1690, Sister of the Visitation & virgin
17 Ignatius of Antioch, 107, bishop & martyr in Rome
18 **Feast: Luke, Evangelist**   Luke 10:1-9
19 Isaac Jogues, SJ, John de Brebeuf, SJ, & Companions, 1640's, martyrs
20 Paul of the Cross, 1775, priest & founder of the Passionists
22 Blessed John Paul II, anniversary of 1978 inauguration
28 **Feast: Simon and Jude, Apostles**   Luke 6:12-16

The glory of God is the human person fully alive.
St. Irenaeus, June 28

Live good lives, and you yourself will be God's praise.
St. Augustine, August 28

A tree gives glory to God by being a tree.
Thomas Merton, December 10

NOVEMBER

1 **Solemnity: All Saints**   Matthew 5:1-12a
2 **All Souls**   Matthew 5:1-12a   Matthew 11:25-30
                     Matthew 25:31-46   Luke 7:11-17   Luke23:44-24:6a
                     Luke 24:13-16,28-35   John 5:24-29   John 6:37-40
                     John 6:51-58   John 11:17-27   Jn 11:32-45   or   Jn 14:1-6
3 Martin de Porres of Lima in Peru, OP, 1639, religious
4 Charles Borromeo, 1584, bishop of Milan
9 **Feast: Dedication of John Lateran Basilica**   John 2:13-22
10 Leo the Great, 461, pope & doctor
11 Martin of Tours, 397, bishop & founder of first monastery in the West
12 Josaphat, 1623, monk, bishop of Polotsk & martyr
13 Frances Xavier Cabrini, 1917, virgin & founder: Sisters of the Sacred Heart
15 Albert the Great, OP, 1280, bishop of Ratisbon & doctor
17 Elizabeth of Hungary,1231, queen & 3rd Order Franciscan
18 Rose Philippine Duchesne, 1852 in St. Louis, Missouri, virgin
21 Presentation of Mary
22 Cecilia, 3rd century(?), virgin & martyr
23 Miguel Agustin Pro, SJ, 1927, priest & martyr in Mexico
24 Andrew Dung-Lac, 1839, priest & 116 Companions, martyrs in Vietnam
25 Catherine of Alexandria, 305(?), virgin & martyr
4th Thursday, Thanksgiving Day (USA)   Luke 10:21-24   or Luke 17:11-19
30 **Feast: Andrew, Apostle**   Matthew 4:18-22

DECEMBER

3 Francis Xavier, SJ, 1552, priest & missionary
4 John of Damascus, 749, priest & doctor
6 Nicholas, 350, bishop of Myra (now in Turkey)
7 Ambrose, 397, bishop of Milan & doctor
8 **Solemnity: Immaculate Conception of Mary**   Luke 1:26-47
9 Juan Diego of Tepayac, Mexico, 1531 apparition of OurLadyOfGuadalupe
12 **Feast: Our Lady of Guadalupe**   Luke 1:26-38 or 39-47
13 Lucy of Syracuse, 304, virgin & martyr
14 John of the Cross, 1591, founder: Discalced Carmelites, priest & doctor
21 Peter Canisius, SJ, 1597, missionary, priest & doctor
25 **Solemnity: Nativity of the Lord**   Vigil: Matthew 1:1-25
   Midnight: Luke 2:1-14   Dawn: Luke 2:15-20   Christmas Day: John 1:1-18
26 **Feast: Stephen, Deacon & First Martyr**   Matthew 10:17-22
27 **Feast: John, Apostle & Evangelist**   John 20:1a,2-8
28 **Feast: The Holy Innocents, Martyrs**   Matthew 2:13-18
29 Thomas Becket, 1170, bishop of Canterbury & martyr

ADVENT

The season of Advent begins the new year of liturgy on the First Sunday of Advent, the Sunday nearest to November 30 (by coincidence the Feast of Saint Andrew), and concludes on the evening of December 24.

SONG A (Choose one.)

Come, Thou long ex-pect-ed Je-sus
Born to set your peo-ple free;
From our fears and sins re-lease us,
Let us find our rest in thee.

Is-rael's strength and con-so-la-tion,
Hope of all the earth you are;
Dear de-sire of ev-'ry na-tion,
Joy of ev-'ry long-ing heart.

Born your peo-ple to de-liv-er,
Born a child and yet a king,
Born to reign in us for-ev-er,
Now your gra-cious king-dom bring.

By your own e-ter-nal Spir-it
Rule in all our hearts a-lone;
By your all suf-fic-ient mer-it,
Raise us to your glo-rious throne.

Text: Charles Wesley, *Hymns for the Nativity of our Lord*, 1745, altered
Music: 87 87 D, STUTTGART, Christian F. Witt, 1715;
adapted by Henry J. Gauntlett, d.1876
Alternate Melody: HYFRYDOL, Rowland H. Prichard, 1830,
Love Divine All Love Excelling

10

SONG B

> **O come**, **O come**, **Em-man**/\\-**u-el**,
> And ran-som cap-tive Is\\\\-ra-el,
> That mourns in lone-ly ex\\-ile here
> Un-til the Son of God/\\ ap-pear.
> *Re-joice! Re-joice! Em-man /\\ -u-el*
> *Shall come to you, O Is \\ \\ -ra-el.*

(17th)

O come now Wis-dom of our God Most High,
With love and ten-der strength,
      Cre-a-tor Guide;
To us the path of true know-ledge show,
And teach us in her sa-ving Way to go.

Rejoice!...

(18th)

O come great Lord of an-cient Is-ra-el,
Who in the fire to Mos-es showed your-self,
And gave the Law up-on Si-nai height;
Stretch out your hand and
      free us by your might.   *Rejoice!...*

(19th)

O come raise up, deep Root of Jes-se's tree,
A sign for peo-ple seek-ing to be free,
Be-fore whom na-tions' rul-ers will bow,
Come save with-out de-lay to keep your vow.

Rejoice!...

(20th)

O come, O Key of Da-vid, Roy-al Pow'r,
And o-pen gates to end our cap-tive hour;
For all be-hind a dark pris-on wall
Re-move the fear that blocks your sac-red call.

Re-joice!...

(21st)

O come, O Ra-diant Dawn, e-ter-nal light,
Come shine and put the fear of death to flight.
In splen-dor o-ver dwell-ings of shade
The sun of Jus-tice has our full debt paid.

Re-joice! *Re-joice! Em-man /\ -u-el*
Shall come to you, O Is \ \ -ra-el.

(22nd)

O come, O King of na-tions, migh-ty arc,
Au-then-tic joy of ev-'ry hu-man heart;
O Key-stone, true foun-da-tion to trust,
Come save us whom you
fash-ion from the dust.

Rejoice!...

(23rd)

O come, de-sire of all the na-tions, bind
In one the hearts and souls of hu-man-kind;
Come make our sad di-vis-ions to cease,
And be, Em-man-u-el, our King of Peace.

Rejoice!...

Text: Combined from O Antiphons, 12th Century?;
translated by John M. Neale, 1851, altered
Music: VENI EMMANUEL, LM with refrain; 15th Century;
adapted by Thomas Helmore, 1856

Advent Psalm   Psalm 85:9ab,10-14

Leader: Come, O Lord,

All: **And set us free.**

12

I will listen to what the Lord God will say,
promising peace to the people.
Surely near to loyal ones is salvation,
the glory to dwell in our land.

Side 2

Love and Faithfulness meet;
Justice and Peace kiss.
Faithfulness springs forth from the earth
and Justice looks down from the heavens.

Side 1

Indeed the Lord will give the good
and our land will yield her harvest,
Justice going forward to prepare
the way for the steps of the Lord.

Side 2

Glory to the Father, and to the Son,
and to the Holy Spirit:

Side 1

As it was in the beginning, is now,
and will be forever. Amen.

Leader: **Come, O Lord,**   All: **And set us free.**

Advent Mondays: Time of Expectation
13ᵗʰ Psalm of Saint Francis

Until when, Lord; will you forget me forever?
Until when will you hide your face from me?
Psalm 13:2

Until when must I wrestle
with thoughts of my soul
and sorrow in my heart day by day?
Ps 13:3a

Until when will enemies triumph?
Look and give answer, Lord, my God.
Ps 13:3b-4a

Give light to my eyes
that no enemy will say, "I overcame that one."
Ps 13:4b-5a

Foes may rejoice when I fall,
but my trust is in your unfailing love.
Ps 13:5b-6a

My heart rejoices in your salvation
and I will sing to the Lord who is good to me.
Ps 13:6bd

Glory to the Father and to the Son
and to the Holy Spirit:

As it was in the beginning, is now,
and will be forever. Amen.

SCRIPTURE AND/OR THE "OUR FATHER"

CLOSING PRAISES, page 102

Advent Tuesdays: Vision of Fulfillment
14ᵗʰ Psalm of Saint Francis

I will praise you, Lord,
Holy Father, Ruler of heaven and earth,
for you have heard me.
Is 12:1; Mt 11:25; Sir 51:1

You are my saving God;
I will trust and will not be afraid.
Ps 25:5b; Is 12:2a

The Lord is my strength and my song
and has become to me salvation.
Is 12:2b; Ex 15:2

Your right hand, O Lord,
magnificent in power,
your right hand, O Lord,
shatters enmity.
Ex 15:6

You poor ones, see and be glad;
may your hearts now live,
you seekers of God.
Ps 69:33ab

For the Lord hears the needy ones
and despises not the captives.
Ps 69:34

Let heaven and earth give praise
with the seas and all moving in them.
Ps 69:35

For God will save Zion
and rebuild the cities of Judah.

Ps 69:36ab

Then they will settle there
and possess her.

Ps 69:36c

The children of the servants will inherit her
and lovers of the Name will dwell in her.

Ps 69:37

Glory to the Father and to the Son
and to the Holy Spirit:

As it was in the beginning, is now,
and will be forever. Amen.

SCRIPTURE AND/OR THE "OUR FATHER"

CLOSING PRAISES, page 102

Advent Wednesdays: Shout of Joy
10ᵗʰ Psalm of Saint Francis

Shout to God all the earth!
Sing the glory of the name!
Offer glory and praise to God!
Ps 66:1-2

Say to God, "How awesome you are;
 how great are your deeds."
Enmity cringes before you and your power.
Ps 66:3

All on the earth bow down to you,
they sing praise to your name,
they sing praise to you.
Ps 66:4

Come! Listen!
Let me tell all who fear God
what God has done for my very self.
Ps 66:16

To God my mouth cried out
with praises on my tongue.
Ps 66:17

I cried for help from my God,
who heard from the temple my voice,
my cry going into those ears.
Ps 18:7cd

Peoples, praise our God!
Make heard the praise!
Ps 66:8

May the name endure to forever
and continue as long as the sun;
being thus blessed, may the nations bless.
Ps 72:17cd

Praised be God, the Lord and God of Israel,
alone doing marvelous deeds.
Ps 72:18; 136:4

Praised be the glory of the name to forever;
may the earth be filled with the glory of God.
Ps 72:19

Glory to the Father and to the Son
and to the Holy Spirit:

As it was in the beginning, is now,
and will be forever. Amen.

SCRIPTURE AND/OR THE "OUR FATHER"

CLOSING PRAISES, page 102

Advent Thursdays: Cry of Hope
11ᵗʰ Psalm of Saint Francis

May the Lord answer you on days of distress;
may the name of the God of Jacob protect you.
Ps 20:2

May God help you from the sanctuary
and support you from Zion.
Ps 20:3

May God remember all of your sacrifices
and accept your burnt offerings.
Ps 20:4

May God give to you as your heart desires
and make all of your plans succeed.
Ps 20:5

We will shout for joy at your victory
and lift a banner in the name of our God.
Ps 20:6

May the Lord grant all your requests.
Ps 20:7ab

Now I know that the Lord sends
the chosen anointed, Jesus Christ the Son,
to judge peoples with justice.

Ps 20:7cd; 9:9b; Jn 3:17

The Lord is the refuge for the oppressed,
the stronghold in times of trouble.
May those who know the Name
trust in the Lord.

Ps 9:10-11a

Blessed be the Lord, my Rock,
my love and fortress, my strong deliverer,
my shield in whom I take refuge.

Ps 144:1b; 59:17cd

To you, my Strength, I sing praise
for you God, my fortress,
you God are my love.

Ps 59:18

Glory to the Father and to the Son
and to the Holy Spirit:

As it was in the beginning, is now,
and will be forever. Amen.

SCRIPTURE AND/OR THE "OUR FATHER"

CLOSING PRAISES, page 102

Advent Fridays: Prayer of a Child
12th Psalm of Saint Francis

In you, Lord, I take refuge;
let me not be shamed to forever.
In your justice you rescue and deliver me.
Ps 71:1b-2a

Turn your ear to me and save me!
Command that I may be saved.
Ps 71:2b,3b

Be to me as a rock
and a refuge to go to always.
Ps 71:3a

For you are my hope, Lord God,
my confidence since my youth.
Ps 71:5

I have relied on you from birth;
my praise is ever to you.
Ps 71:6

May my mouth be filled all the day
with praise of your splendor.
Ps 71:8

Answer me, Lord, for good is your love!
In your great mercies, turn to me!
Ps 69:17

Hide not your face from your servant;
to my trouble, be quick to answer me.
Ps 69:18

Blessed be the Lord, my Rock,
my love and fortress, my strong deliverer,
my shield in whom I take refuge.

Ps 144:1b; 59:17cd

To you, my Strength, I sing praise
for you God, my fortress,
you God are my love.

Ps 59:18

    Glory to the Father and to the Son
    and to the Holy Spirit:

    As it was in the beginning, is now,
    and will be forever. Amen.

SCRIPTURE AND/OR THE "OUR FATHER"

CLOSING PRAISES, page 102

CHRISTMAS

Christmas Day is always on December 25. The season of Christmas begins the evening before (the 24th), and concludes on the evening of the Feast of the Baptism of the Lord.

SONG A (Choose one.)

An-gels we have heard on high
Sweet-ly sing-ing o'er the plains,
And the moun-tains in re-ply
E-cho back their joy-ous strains.
Refrain   Glo/\\\//\\\//\\\/-ri-a in ex-cel-sis De-o!
Glo/\\\//\\\//\\\/-ri-a in ex-cel-sis De\-o!

Text: French, 18th C.; tr. From *Crown of Jesus Music, II,* London, 1862.
Music: 77 77 GLORIA with refrain, traditional French carol

SONG B   **O come, all ye faith-ful**,
joy-ful and tri-um-phant,
O come ye, O come/ ye,
to Beth\-le-hem.
Come and be-hold him,
born the King of an\-gels;
O come, let us a-dore him,
O come, let us a-dore him,
O come, let us a-dore him/,
Christ \ the Lord.

Text: John f. Wade, 1743; translated by Frederick Oakeley, 1841
Music: ADESTE FIDELES, attributed variously to
John Wade, John Reading, or Simon Portogallo

SONG C

Hark! the her-ald an-gels sing\,
"Glo-ry to the new-born King;
Peace on earth and mer-cy mild\,
God and sin-ners re-con-ciled!"
Joy-ful, all ye na-tions rise\,
Join the tri-umph of the skies\;
With th'an-gel-ic host pro-claim.
"Christ is/ born in Beth-le-hem!"
Hark! the her-ald an-gels sing,
"Glo-ry / to the new-born King!"

Text: see Luke 2:14; Charles Wesley, 1739
Music: 7777777777 MENDELSSOHN, Felix Mendelssohn, 1840

SONG D

O sanc-tis-si-ma/, O pi-is-si-ma/,
Dul-cis vir-go Ma-ri\-a!
Ma/-ter a-ma/-ta, In/ te-me-ra/-ta,
O\-ra\, O\-ra\ pro-no\-bis.

Ho-ly, ho-ly Ma-ry,
Hum-ble strength of Ma-ry,
Sweet-ness, vir-gin Ma-ri\-a!
Moth-er of our Sa/-vior,
In your fi-at "yes" and more,
O\-ra\, O\-ra\, pray\ for us.

Text: *Stimmen der Volker in Liedern*, 1807
Music: 55 7 55 7, O DU FROLICHE; Tattersall's *Improved Psalmody*, 1704

Christmas Psalm
Psalm 98:1-6

Leader: All the ends of the earth…

All: **Have seen the power of God.**

Side 1 (Leader's side)
Sing a new song to the Lord
who has done marvelous things,
working salvation at the right hand
and by the holy arm.

Side 2
The Lord has made known salvation,
justice revealed for the eyes of nations.
Love is remembered and faithfulness
to the house of Israel.

1

All the ends of the earth can see
the salvation of our God.
Shout for joy to the Lord, all you earth!
Burst forth and sing; make music!

2

Make music to the Lord with harp,
with harp and the sound of singing,
with trumpets and blast of a ram horn:
shout for joy before the King, the Lord!

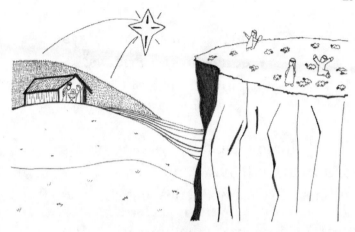

1

Glory to the Father, and to the Son,
and to the Holy Spirit:

2

As it was in the beginning, is now,
and will be forever. Amen.

Leader: All the ends of the earth…

All: **Have seen the power of God.**

Christmas Sundays, Mondays,
Wednesdays, & Fridays:
Origin and Birth of Christ
15th Psalm of Saint Francis

Sing for joy to God our strength;
turn to God, living and true.
Shout to God with cries of joy!
Ps 81:2a; 1 Th 1:9; Ps 47:2

How awesome is the Lord Most High,
the great King over all the earth.
Ps 47:3

Our Father of heaven and earth,
the King before all the ages,
sent from heaven the Beloved Begotten Son
to be born of the Blessed Virgin Mary.
Ps 74:12a; 144:7; Ga 4:4; Creed

The Son called out: "you are my Father,"
who appointed him as the firstborn
and most exalted above kings of the earth.
Ps 89:27a,28

On that day the Lord sent Merciful Love
and at night the song within us.
Ps 42:9ab

This is the day the Lord has made;
let us rejoice and be glad.
Ps 118:24

A child is born to us, a Son is given to us,
born to us on the way and laid in a manger
because there was no place in the inn.
Is 9:5; Lk 2:7,12,16

Glory to God on high
and on earth peace to people of good will.
Lk 2:14

Let the heavens rejoice and the earth be glad;
let the sea resound and all its fullness;
let the fields and all that is in them be jubilant.
Ps 96:11-12a

Sing to the Lord a new song!
Sing to the Lord, all the earth!
Ps 96:1

For the Lord is great, greatly being praised,
the one held in awe above all so-called "gods."
Ps 96:4

Bring to the Lord, families of nations,
bring to the Lord glory and strength,
bring to the Lord the glory of the name.
Ps 96:7-8a

> **G**lory to the Father and to the Son
> and to the Holy Spirit:
>
> **A**s it was in the beginning, is now,
> and will be forever. Amen.

SCRIPTURE AND/OR THE "OUR FATHER"

CLOSING PRAISES, page 102

JANUARY

(after the Baptism of the Lord)

SONG A (Choose one.)

On Jor-dan's bank the Bap-tist's cry
An-nounc-es that the Lord is nigh;
A-wake and heark-en, for he brings
Glad ti-dings of the King of kings.

Then cleansed be ev-'ry soul from sin;
Make straight the way of God with-in,
Pre-pare we in our hearts a home,
Where such a migh-ty guest may come.

For you are our sal-va-tion, Lord,
Our ref-uge and our sure re-ward;
Shine forth, and let your light re-store
Our souls to heav'n-ly grace once more.

All praise, e-ter-nal Son, to thee
Whose ad-vent set your peo-ple free,
Whom with the Fa-ther we a-dore
And Ho-ly Spir-it ev-er-more.

Text: Charles Coffin, d.1749; translated by John Chandler, d.1876, altered
Music: WINCHESTER NEW, CM, *Musikalisches Handbuch*, Hamburg, 1690;
adapted by William H. Havergal, d.1870

SONG B

Cre-a-tor of the stars of night,
Your peo-ple's ev-er-last-ing light,
Re-deem-er Je-sus, save us all,
And hear your ser-vants when we call.

You griev-ing that the an-cient curse
Should doom to death a u-niv-erse,
Find now the med-i-cine of grace,
To save and heal the hu-man race.

See now the Bride-groom of the bride,
As drew the world to eve-ning tide;
Pro-ceed-ing from a vir-gin shrine,
As ful-ly hu-man and div-ine.

This Awe-some Name, ma-jes-tic now,
All knees to bend and hearts to bow;
All things ce-les-tial God does own,
And things ter-res-trial, God a-lone.

To God the Fa-ther, God the Son,
And God the Spir-it, Three in One,
Laud, ho-nor, might, and glo-ry be
From age to age e-ter-nal-ly.

Text: 7th Century unknown author; trans. by John M. Neale, 1852, altered
Music: CONDITOR, LM; *Conditor Alme Siderum,* Sarum plainsong, Mode IV

January Psalm

Psalm 72:2,7-8,10-13

Leader: Lord, all peoples and every nation,

All: **All the earth will adore you.**

Side 1 (Leader's side)

O God, endow your justice to the king,
and your judgment to the son of the king;
may he judge your people in righteousness
and your afflicted with justice.

Side 2

In his days the righteous will flourish,
prosperous abundance til the moon is no more.
He will rule from sea to sea
and from the river to the ends of the earth.

1

The kings of Tarshish and the distant shores
will bring tribute and present gifts,
with kings of Sheba and Seba.
They will bow down to him;
all the kings of the nations will thus serve.

2

For he will deliver the needy one crying out
and the afflicted one when no one is helping.
He will take pity on the weak and the needy
and will save the lives of the needy ones.

1

Glory to the Father, and to the Son,
and to the Holy Spirit:

2

As it was in the beginning, is now,
and will be forever. Amen.

Leader: Lord, all peoples and every nation,

All: **All the earth will adore you.**

ORDINARY TIME COMMONS PSALM:

Apostles	Sundays	page 88
Martyrs	Mondays	page 90
Holy Women	Tuesdays	page 92
Pastors & Doctors	Wednesdays	page 94
Holy Men	Thursdays	page 96
Virgins	Fridays	page 98
Mary	Saturdays	page 100

FEBRUARY

(until Ash Wednesday)

SONG A (Choose one.)

Faith of our an-ces-tors, liv\-ing still,
In spite of dun-geon, fire\ and sword;
O how our hearts\ beat high\ with joy
When-'er we hear that glo/-rious Word!
Faith of our an-ces-tors, ho-ly faith!
We will be true to you till death.

Faith of our **fa\-thers**, we\ will strive
A-mong all peo-ples, as is our call;
That thru the truth\ that comes\ from God,
True free-dom may be found/ by all.
Faith of our an-ces-tors, ho-ly faith!
We will be true to you till death.

Faith of our **mo\-thers**, we\ will love
Both friend and foe in all\ our strife;
Liv-ing and preach-ing as love\ knows how
By kind-ly words and vir/-tuous life.
Faith of our an-ces-tors, ho-ly faith!
We will be true to you till death.

Text: Frederick W. Faber, *Jesus and Mary*, 1849;
refrain by James G. Walton, 1874; altered
Music: ST. CATHERINE, LM with refrain; Henry F. Hemy, 1864;
adapted by James G. Walton, 1874

SONG B

Shep-herd of souls, re-fresh and bless
Your cho-sen pil-grim flock
With man-na in the wil-der-ness,
And wa-ter from the rock.

Hung-ry and thirs-ty, mor-tal, weak,
As you would come and go:
Our souls the joys of heav-en seek
Which from your pass-ion flow.

We would not live by bread a-lone,
But by your Word of grace,
In strength of which we trav-el on
To our a-bi-ding place.

Be known to us in break-ing bread,
But do not then de-part;
Sa-vior, a-bide with us and spread
Your ta-ble in our heart.

Text: James Mongtomery, 1825, altered
Music: ST. AGNES, CM, John B. Dykes, 1866

February Canticle   Revelation 15:3b-4

Leader: Sion, sing, break into song!

All: **The Lord is with you.**

Side 1 (Leader's side)

Great and wonderful are your works,
Lord God Almighty.
Just and true are your ways,
King of the nations.

Side 2

Who will not fear you, O Lord,
or glorify your name?

1

Only you are holy.
All the nations will come
and worship before you;
your orderings are shown to all.

2

Glory to the Father, and to the Son,
and to the Holy Spirit:

1

As it was in the beginning, is now,
and will be forever. Amen.

Leader: Sion, sing, break into song!

All: **The Lord is with you.**

ORDINARY TIME COMMONS PSALM:

LENT

The season of Lent begins with Ash Wednesday, six and one half weeks prior to Easter Sunday.

SONG A (Choose one.)

> **For-ty days and for-ty nights**
> You were fast-ing in the wild;
> For-ty days and for-ty nights
> Temp-ted, and yet un-de-filed.
>
> Should not we your sor-row share
> And from world-ly joys ab-stain,
> Fast-ing with un-ceas-ing prayer,
> Strong with you to suf-fer pain?
>
> When temp-ta-tions on us press,
> Je-sus, Sa-vior, hear our call!
> Vic-tor in the wil-der-ness,
> Grant we may not faint nor fall!
>
> Keep, O keep us, Sa-vior dear,
> Ev-er con-stant by your side;
> That with you we may ap-pear
> At th'e-ter-nal Eas-ter-tide.

Text: George H. Smyttan, *The Penny Post,* 1856, altered
Music: 7 7 7 7 HEINLEIN, Attributed to Martin Herbst, d. 1681

SONG B

When/ I sur\-vey the/ won-drous cross
On which the Prince of glo-ry died,
My rich-est/ gain\ I count\ as loss,
And pour con-tempt on all my pride.

For/-bid it\, Lord, that/ I should boast,
Save in the death of Christ my God!
May all vain/ things\ that charm\ me most,
Be sac-ri-ficed as with his blood.

Were/ the whole\ realm of/ na-ture mine,
That trea-sure would be far too small;
Love so a/-ma\-zing, so\ div-ine,
De-mands my soul, my life, my all.

Text: Isaac Watts, *Hymns and Spiritual Songs*, 1707, altered
Music option: ERHALT UNS HERR, LM; Klug's *Geistliche Lieder, 1543;*
Popular melody for: *The Glory Of These Forty Days*

Lent Canticle   Philippians 2:6-11

Leader: With the Lord…

All: **There is mercy.**

Side 1 (Leader's side)

Christ Jesus, subsisting in the form of God,
did not deem equality with God
something to grab,
but emptied himself, taking the form of a slave,
becoming in human likeness.

Side 2

And being found in human fashion,
he humbled himself,
becoming obedient until death,
and death on a cross.

1

And so God highly exalted him,
and gave to him the name above every name,
that in the name of Jesus
every knee should bend,
of heavenly beings and earthly beings,
and beings under the earth;

2

And every tongue acknowledge
to the glory of God the Father
that Jesus Christ is Lord.

1

Glory to the Father, and to the Son,
and to the Holy Spirit:

2

As it was in the beginning, is now,
and will be forever. Amen.

Leader: With the Lord…

All: **There is mercy.**

Lent Mondays: Gethsemane
1st Psalm of Saint Francis

O God, my laments are in your record
and my tears are in your wineskin.
Ps 56:9

Together against me they whisper,
imagining the worst for me;
waiting on my life, they conspire together.
Ps 41:8a; 71:10c

They repay good with evil
and hatred for my friendship.
Ps 109:5

In return for my friendship
they accuse me, but I pray:
Ps 109:4ab

Be not far from me
my holy Father, king of heaven and earth,
for trouble is near with no one to help.
Mt 26:42; Jn 17:11; Ps 22:12

Those who would be enemies
will turn back on the day I call;
I will know that God is for me.
Ps 56:10

My friends and companions from the past
avoid being present to my woundedness,
and my neighbors stay far away.
Ps 38:12

Holy Father, be not far off;
come quickly to help me, my Strength!

Jn 17:11; Ps 22:20

Come quickly to my help,
Lord of my salvation.

Ps 38:23

Glory to the Father and to the Son
and to the Holy Spirit:

As it was in the beginning, is now,
and will be forever. Amen.

SCRIPTURE AND/OR THE "OUR FATHER"

CLOSING PRAISES, page 102

Lent Tuesdays: The Sanhedrin
2nd Psalm of Saint Francis

Lord God, my Savior,
I cry out day and night before you.
Ps 88:2

May my prayer come before you;
turn your ear to my cry.
Ps 88:3

Come near because of enmity;
rescue my soul and redeem me!
Ps 69:19; 30:2

You brought me out from the womb,
to trust in you at the breast of my mother.
From the womb I was cast upon you.
Ps 22:10-11a

From my very birth, you are my God;
be not far from me.
Ps 22:11b-12

You know my scorn
and shame and disgrace,
and you know my reverence.
Ps 69:20a

Enmity is in your sight before you;
scorn broke my heart
and I became helpless.
Ps 69:20b-21a

I looked to have sympathy
but there was none,
and for comforters,
but found none.
Ps 69:21b-d

Arrogant ones attack against me, God;
a band of ruthless people seek my life
and they do not look to see you.
Ps 86:14

I am being counted
with those going down the pit,
like a human with no strength
as set apart with the dead.
Ps 88:5-6a

You are my Holy Father,
my King and my God.
Ps 89:27; 44:5a

Come quickly to my help,
Lord of my salvation.
Ps 38:23

Glory to the Father and to the Son
and to the Holy Spirit:

As it was in the beginning, is now,
and will be forever. Amen.

SCRIPTURE AND/OR THE "OUR FATHER"

CLOSING PRAISES, page 102

Lent Thursdays: Pontius Pilate
4ᵗʰ Psalm of Saint Francis

Be merciful to me, my God!
Human beings pursue me all the day,
attacking with oppression and with slander.
Ps 56:2

Indeed in their pride
do the many attack me.
Ps 56:3

Enemies ask in malice,
"When will that one die and the name perish?"
When they come to see me they speak
with false hearts to gather slander.
Ps 41:8b-9a

Enemies speak against me
and, waiting on my life, conspire together.
Ps 71:10b

Then they go out to the outside to speak
and whisper together against me.
Ps 41:7

All those seeing me mock me;
they shake their heads in insult.
Ps 22:8

Treated like a worm and not human,
I am the scorn of humanity,
despised by people.
Ps 22:7

The utter contempt of even my neighbors,
I am a dread to my friends
who see me on the street and flee.
Ps 31:12ab

Holy Father, be not far off;
come quickly to help me, my Strength!
Jn 17:11; Ps 22:20

Come quickly to my help,
Lord of my salvation.
Ps 38:23

> Glory to the Father and to the Son
> and to the Holy Spirit:
>
> As it was in the beginning, is now,
> and will be forever. Amen.

SCRIPTURE AND/OR THE "OUR FATHER"

CLOSING PRAISES, page 102

Lent Fridays: The Cross
5th Psalm of Saint Francis

My voice asks for mercy,
my voice cries to the Lord.
Ps 142:2

Before whom I pour out my complaint,
before whom I tell my trouble.
Ps 142:3

When my spirit grows faint within me
then you know my way.
Ps 142:4ab

In the path where I walk
they hid a snare for me.
Ps 142:4cd

Look right and see:
the one with concern for me
has fled away from me for refuge.
Ps 142:5ab

There is no one who cares for my life.
Ps 142:5cd

For your sake I endure scorn
and shame covers my face.
Ps 69:8

I am a stranger to my brothers and sisters,
an alien to the children of my mother.
Ps 69:9

Holy Father,
zeal for you house consumes me
and insults of your insulters fall on me.
Jn 17:11; Ps 69:10

They took glee at my stumbling
and they gathered and gathered attackers
and did not cease to slander.
Ps 35:15

Those hating me for no reason
are more numerous
than the hairs of my head.
Ps 69:5ab

more

Many are the ones destroying me,
those who would be enemies for no reason.
What I did not steal I must restore.
Ps 69:5cd

Ruthless witnesses come forward;
on things I cannot know
they question me.
Ps 35:11

They repay me evil for good;
they slander me when I seek the good.
Ps 35:12a; 38:21

You are my Holy Father,
my King and my God.
Ps 44:5

Come quickly to my help,
Lord of my salvation.
Ps 38:23

Glory to the Father and to the Son
and to the Holy Spirit:

As it was in the beginning, is now,
and will be forever. Amen.

SCRIPTURE AND/OR THE "OUR FATHER"

CLOSING PRAISES, page 102

Lent Saturdays: Death on the Cross
6ᵗʰ Psalm of Saint Francis

All of you passing by the way,
consider and see
if there is a sorrow like my sorrow.
Lam 1:12ab

Dogs indeed surround around me,
a band of bad doers
encircles me as a lion.
Ps 22:17

They stare and they gloat over me;
they divide my garments among them
and for my clothing they cast lots.
Ps 22:18b,19

They make ready
to tear into my hands and my feet;
I can count all of my bones.
Ps 22:17c-18a

They open wide their mouths against me,
lions tearing up prey and roaring.
Ps 22:14

Like the waters I am poured out
and my bones are all out of joint.
Ps 22:15ab

My heart like wax
melts away within my insides.
Ps 22:15c

Like a broken clay pot, my strength is dried up;
my tongue is stuck in the roof of my mouth.

Ps 22:16ab

They put gall in my food
and for my thirst
they gave me vinegar to drink.

Ps 69:22

They lay me in the dust of death
and talk about the pain of hurt.

Ps 22:16c; 69:27b

I lie down and I sleep, and wake up again;
my Holy Father takes me after the glory.

Ps 3:6; 73:24c

Holy Father,
you hold me by my right hand
and with your counsel you guide me
and take me after the glory.

Jn 17:11; Ps 73:24

Who in the heavens is for me?
With you, nothing on earth do I desire.

Ps 73:25

Behold, behold, for I am God,
says the Lord.
I will be exalted among the nations;
I will be exalted on the earth.

see Ps 2:7; Ps 46:11b

Blessed be the Lord the God of Israel,
who redeems with his own blood
the servants of the Lord
and will not abandon
any who take this refuge.

Lk 1:68a; Ps 72:18a;
Ps 34:23a; Heb 9:12

We know that the Son of God
comes and will come to judge justice.

1 Jn 5:20; Ps 96:13b; 75:3

Glory to the Father and to the Son
and to the Holy Spirit:

As it was in the beginning, is now,
and will be forever. Amen.

SCRIPTURE AND/OR THE "OUR FATHER"

CLOSING PRAISES, page 102

EASTER

The Season of Easter begins on the Vigil of Easter Sunday, the first Sunday after the first full moon following the vernal equinox, the first day of Spring.

SONG A (Choose one.)

We walk by faith, and not by sight;
No gra-cious words we hear
From him who spoke as none e'er spoke;
But we be-lieve him near.

We may not touch his hands and side,
Nor fol-low where he trod;
But in his prom-ise we re-joice,
And cry, "My Lord and God!"

Help then, O Lord, our un-be-lief;
And may our faith a-bound,
To call on you when you are near
And seek where you are found.

That, when our life of faith is done,
In realms of clear-er light
We may be-hold you as you are,
With full and end-less sight.

Text: CM, based on 2 Cor. 5:7 and John 20:24-29;
Henry Alford, 1844, altered
Music: ST. AGNES, CM; John B. Dykes, 1866;
Popular melody for: *Shepherd of Souls*
Current familiar tune: SHANTI, by Marty Haugen, GIA Publications, 1984

SONG B

Ye sons and daugh**-ters** of\ the King,
With heav'n-ly hosts\ in glo\-ry sing,
To-day the grave\ has lost\ its sting: *Al-le-lu-ia!*

On that first morn\-ing of\ the week,
Be-fore the day\ be-gan\ to break,
The Ma-rys went\ their Lord\ to seek: *Al-le-lu-ia!*

An an-gel bade\ their sor\-row flee,
By speak-ing thus\ un-to\ the three:
"Your Lord is gone\ to Gal\-i-lee:"   *Al-le-lu-ia!*

That night th'A-pos\-tles met\ in fear,
A-midst them came\ their Lord\ most dear
And said, "Peace be\ un-to\ you here:"*Al-le-lu-ia!*

Bless-ed are they\ that have\ not seen
And yet whose faith\ has con\-stant been,
In life e-ter\-nal they\ shall reign: *Al-le-lu-ia!*

And we with ho\-ly Church\ u-nite,
As ev-er-more\ is just\ and right,
In glo-ry to\ the King\ of light: *Al-le-lu-ia!*

Al-le-lu-ia\! Al-le\-lu-ia! Al-le-lu-ia!

Text: see John 20; attrib. to Jean Tisserand, d. 1494;
translated by John M. Neal, 1851, altered
Music: 888, O FILII ET FILIAE; Chant Mode II,
Airs sur les hymnes sacrez, odes et noels, 1623

Easter Canticle   Revelation 19:1b,2a,3b,5b,6b,7

Leader: Alleluia, alleluia, alleluia.

All: **Alleluia, alleluia, alleluia.**

Side 1 (Leader's side)

Alleluia! Praise the Lord!
Salvation and glory and power are to our God,
whose judgments are true and just.

Side 2

Alleluia! Praise the Lord!
Praise our God, all you servants of the Lord,
you small and you great,
who hold God in awe.

1

Alleluia! Praise the Lord!
The Lord is reigning, our God, the Almighty.
Let us rejoice and let us exalt,
and we will give the glory to the Lord.

2

Alleluia! Praise the Lord!
The day has come
for the marriage of the Lamb,
and the bride has prepared herself.

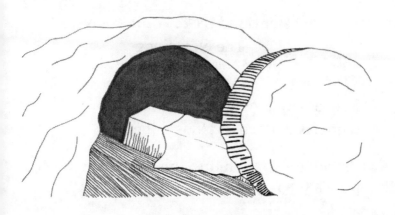

1

Glory to the Father, and to the Son,
and to the Holy Spirit:

2

As it was in the beginning, is now,
and will be forever. Amen.

All: **Alleluia, alleluia, alleluia.**

Easter Sundays & Wednesdays:
The New Song
9th Psalm of Saint Francis

Sing a new song to the Lord
who has done marvelous things,
Ps 98:1ab

Working salvation through the Beloved Son,
his right hand and holy arm.
Ps 98:1cd

The Lord has made known salvation,
justice revealed for the eyes of the nations.
Ps 98:2

On that day the Lord sent Merciful Love
and at night the song within us.
Ps 42:9ab

This is the day the Lord has made;
let us rejoice and be glad.
Ps 118:24

Blessed is the one coming
in the name of the Lord;
our Lord God has shined light onto us.
Ps 118:26a,27a

Let the heavens rejoice.
Let the earth be glad.
Let the sea resound and all its fullness.
Let the fields and all that is in them be jubilant.
Ps 96:11-12a

Bring to the Lord, families of nations,
bring to the Lord glory and strength,
bring to the Lord the glory of the name!

Ps 96:7-8a

From Ascension to Pentecost, add:

Kingdoms of the earth, sing to God!
Sing praise to the Lord!

Ps 68:33a

To the Rider in the skies,
the ancient skies, see!
The voice thunders, the voice of might.

Ps 68:33b-34a

Proclaim the power of God over Israel,
the majesty and power in the skies.

Ps 68:34b-35

Awesome are you, God, in your sanctuary;
the God of Israel gives power and strength
to the people praising God.

Ps 68:36

Glory to the Father and to the Son
and to the Holy Spirit:

As it was in the beginning, is now,
and will be forever. Amen.

SCRIPTURE AND/OR THE "OUR FATHER"

CLOSING PRAISES, page 102

Advent & Lent Sundays,
Easter Mondays & Thursdays:
Acclamation of the Christ
7th Psalm of Saint Francis

All you nations, clap your hands!
Shout to God with cries of joy!
Ps 47:2

How awesome is the Lord Most High,
the great King over all the earth.
Ps 47:3

Our Father of heaven and earth,
our King before all ages,
sent from heaven the Beloved Begotten Son
and brought about salvation
in the center of creation.
Ps 74:12; 144:7; Mt 17:5;
Jn 3:17; Gal 4:4; Creed

Let the heavens rejoice and the earth be glad;
let the sea resound and all its fullness;
let the fields and all that is in them be jubilant.
Ps 96:11-12a

Sing to the Lord a new song!
Sing to the Lord, all the earth!
Ps 96:1

For the Lord is great, greatly being praised,
the one held in awe beyond all so-called "*gods*."
Ps 96:4

Take up his holy cross,
follow his most holy commands,
and abide in him.

Mt 16:24; cf. Jn 15:10

In Advent this psalm ends here.

Worship the Lord in holy splendor!
Tremble in the presence all the earth!
Say among the nations,
"The Lord reigns!"

Ps 96:9b-10a

He ascended into heaven and is seated
at the right hand of God the Father almighty.

Apostles' Creed

Be exalted, God, above the heavens,
your glory over all the earth.

Ps 57:12

We know that the Son of God
comes and will come to judge justice.

1 Jn 5:20; Ps 96:13b; 75:3

Glory to the Father and to the Son
and to the Holy Spirit:

As it was in the beginning, is now,
and will be forever. Amen.

SCRIPTURE AND/OR THE "OUR FATHER"

CLOSING PRAISES, page 102

Christmas Thursdays,
Easter Tuesdays & Fridays:
Echoes of Struggle & Victory
8th Psalm of Saint Francis

O God, save me;
hasten, Lord, to help me.
Ps 70:2

May plans to seek my life
be shamed and confused.
Ps 70:3a

May the desire for my ruin
be turned back in disgrace.
Ps 70:3b

May the ones saying, "aha!, aha!"
turn back in shame.
Ps 70:4

May all who seek you
rejoice in you and be glad.
Ps 70:5a

May lovers of salvation say always,
"Let God be exalted."
Ps 70:5b

Yet I am poor and needy, God;
come quickly.
Ps 70:6a

My help and deliverer, Lord, do not delay.
Ps 70:6b

Glory to the Father and to the Son
and to the Holy Spirit:

As it was in the beginning, is now,
and will be forever. Amen.

SCRIPTURE AND/OR THE "OUR FATHER"

CLOSING PRAISES, page 102

Lent Wednesdays,
Advent & Easter Saturdays,
Christmas Tuesdays & Saturdays:
Morning Sun

3rd Psalm of Saint Francis

Have mercy on me, God,
have mercy on me,
for in you my soul takes refuge.

Ps 57:2a

And in the shade of your wings
I take refuge until disasters pass.

Ps 57:2b

I cry out to God Most High,
to God who fulfills me.

Ps 57:3

God sends from the heavens and saves me
and rebukes the one pursuing me.

Ps 57:4ab

God sends love and fidelity
and rescues me from enmity,
from those too strong for me.

Ps 57:4c-5a; 18:18

For my feet they spread a net
and my self was bowed down.

Ps 57:ab

Before me they dug a pit
and fell into it themselves.

Ps 57:cd

My heart is steadfast, God,
my heart is steadfast;
I will sing and make music.

Ps 57:8

Awake, my glory,
wake up the harp and lyre;
I will wake up the dawn.

Ps 57:9

I will praise you among the nations, Lord;
I will sing of you among the peoples.

Ps 57:10

For great to the heavens is your love
and to the skies is your fidelity.

Ps 57:11

Be exalted above the heavens, God,
your glory over all the earth.

Ps 57:12

Glory to the Father and to the Son
and to the Holy Spirit:

As it was in the beginning, is now,
and will be forever. Amen.

SCRIPTURE AND/OR THE "OUR FATHER"

CLOSING PRAISES, page 102

64

JUNE

(after Pentecost)

SONG A (Choose one.)

O/ breathe on me, O/ breath of God,
Fill/ me with life a//-new,
That I may love what you have loved,
And do what you would do.

O/ breathe on me, O/ breath of God,
Un/-til my heart is// pure,
Un-til with you I will one will,
To do and to en-dure.

O/ breathe on me, O/ breath of God,
In/-spire my bu-sy// mind,
Un-til this earth-ly part of me
Glows with your fire div-ine.

O/ breathe on me, O/ breath of God,
My/ soul shall nev-er// die,
But live in your e-ter-nal life,
Your love the rea-son why.

Text: Edwin Hatch, 1878, altered
Music: ST. COLUMBA, CM; Gaelic Folk Melody
Popular melody for: *The King Of Love My Shepherd Is*

SONG B

Je-sus, my Lord\, **my God**/, **my all**\;
How late, my Je-sus, have I sought.
You pour down rich\-es of/ your grace\;
How can I love you as I ought?
Je-sus, our Lord, we you a-dore!
Call us to love you more/ and more\.
Call us to love you more and more.

Je-sus, what could you have found/ in me\?
How great the joy that you have brought!
How have you dealt\ so pa/-tient-ly\?
So far ex-ceed-ing hope or thought!
Je-sus, our Lord, we you a-dore!
Call us to love you more/ and more\.
Call us to love you more and more.

Had I but Ma\-ry's sin/-less heart\
With which to love you, dear-est King;
O! with what bursts\ of fer/-vent praise\
Your good-ness, Je-sus, would I sing.
Sweet Sac-ra-ment, we you a-dore!
Call us to love you more/ and more\.
Call us to love you more and more.

Text: Henry A. Collins, 1854, altered;
vs. 3 Frederick W. Faber, d. 1863, altered
Music: SWEET SACRAMENT, LM with refrain,
Romischkatholisches Gesanguchlein , 1826

June Psalm   Psalm 104:1ab,24ac,29bc-30,31,34

Leader: Lord, send out your Spirit…

All: **And renew the face of the earth.**

Side 1 (Leader's side)

Bless the Lord, my soul!
Lord, my God, you are beyond measure.
How many are your works, Lord!
The earth is full of your creatures.

Side 2

If you take away their breath they die
and to their dust they return.
You breathe your Spirit, and they are created,
and you renew the faces of earth.

1

May the glory of the Lord endure to forever;
may the Lord rejoice in the works.
May my meditation be found pleasing;
I rejoice in the Lord.

2

Glory to the Father, and to the Son,
and to the Holy Spirit:

1

As it was in the beginning, is now,
and will be forever. Amen.

Leader: Lord, send out your Spirit...

All: **And renew the face of the earth.**

ORDINARY TIME COMMONS PSALM:

J U L Y

SONG A (Choose one.)

In/ Christ there is no/ East or West,
In him no South\ or/ North;
But/ one com-mu-nion of God's love
Through/-out/ the whole\ wide earth.

In/ Christ shall true hearts/ ev-'ry-where
Their high vo-ca\-tion/ find;
His/ ser-vice is the gold-en cord,
Close/ bind/-ing hu\-man-kind.

Join/ hands, then, mem-bers/ of the faith,
What-e'r your race\ may/ be!
Who/ serves my Fa-ther as his child
Is/ sure/-ly kin\ to me.

In/ Christ now meet both/ East and West,
In him meet South\ and/ North;
All/ souls of Christ are one in him
Through/-out/ the whole\ wide earth.

Text: see Galatians 3:8; William A. Dunkerley, 1908, under
the pseudonym of John Oxenham, altered
Music: MCKEE, CM; African American Spiritual,
arranged by Harry T. Burleigh, 1866-1949

SONG B

God, whose farm is all cre-a-tion,
Take the grat-i-tude we give;
Take the fi-nest of our har-vest,
Crops we grow so peo-ple live.

Take our plow-ing, seed-ing, reap-ing,
Hopes and fears of sun and rain,
All our think-ing, plan-ning, wait-ing,
Ri-pened in new fruit and grain.

All our la-bor, all our watch-ing,
All our cal-en-dar of care,
In all crops of your cre-a-tion,
Take, O God, they are our prayer.

Text: John Arlott, 1914, altered
Music: 87 87 D, STUTTGART, Christian F. Witt, 1715;
adapted by Henry J. Gauntlett, d.1876
Popular melody for: *Come Thou Long Expected Jesus*

July Canticle   Ephesians 1:3-10

Leader: As the Father has sent me so I send you...

All: **Peace be with you.**

Side 1 (Leader's side)

Blessed be the God and Father
of our Lord Jesus Christ,
who has blessed us in Christ
with every spiritual blessing in the heavens.

Side 2

God chose us in Christ
before the foundation of the world,
to be holy and free of blemish before him.

1

In love, God gave us a destiny:
as sons are adopted,
through Jesus Christ himself,
in accord with the good pleasure of God's will
to the praise of the glory of grace
by which we are favored as God's beloved.

2

In Christ we have the redemption
through his blood, the forgiveness of sins,
in accord with the riches of his grace
which he made abound to us.

1

In all wisdom and intelligence
the mystery of God's will is made known to us
in accord with God's good pleasure
and purpose:

2

A stewardship of the fullness of time,
heading up all things in Christ,
the things in the heavens
and the things on earth.

1

Glory to the Father, and to the Son,
and to the Holy Spirit:

2

As it was in the beginning, is now,
and will be forever. Amen.

Leader: As the Father has sent me so I send you...

All: **Peace be with you.**

ORDINARY TIME COMMONS PSALM:

AUGUST

SONG A (Choose one.)

Come, Ho-ly Spir-it, who ev-er One
Are with the Fa\-ther and/ the Son;
Come, Ho-ly Spir-it, our souls pos-sess
With your full flood of\ ho-li-ness;
With your full flood of\ ho-li-ness.

In will and deed-, by heart and tongue,
With all our pow-ers, your praise/ be sung;
Light up in love our hu-man frame,
Till oth-ers catch the\ liv-ing flame;
Till oth-ers catch the\ liv-ing flame.

Fa-ther Al-migh-ty, hear now our cry
Through Je-sus Christ\ our Lord/ most high,
Who with the Ho-ly Spir-it and Thee
Do live and reign e\-ter-nal-ly;
Do live and reign e\-ter-nal-ly.

Text: attributed to Ambrose of Milan, *Nunc Sancte nobis Spiritus*, d.397;
translated by John Henry Newman, *Tracts for the Times*, 1836, altered
Music: LAMBILLOTTE, LM; with repeat; Louis Lambillotte, SJ, 1796-1855
Popular melody for: *Come, Holy Ghost, Creator Blest...*

SONG B

My life flows on in end-less song
A-bove earth's lam-en-ta-tion.
I hear that near and far-off hymn,
It heals a new cre-a-tion:
Thru all the tu-mult and the strife
I hear that mu-sic ring-ing;
It finds an ech-o\ in my soul;
How can I keep from sing-ing?

What though my joys and com-forts fade
The Lord my Sa-vior liv-eth;
What though the shad-ows gath-er round
Songs in the night he giv-eth:
No storm can shake my in-most calm,
While to that ref-uge cling-ing;
Since Christ is Lord of\ heav'n and earth,
How can I keep from sing-ing?

I lift my eyes; the clouds grow thin;
I see the blue a-bove it;
And day by day clears way the path
Since first I learned to love it:
The peace of Christ makes fresh my heart,
A foun-tain ev-er spring-ing;
All things are mine since\ I am his;
How can I keep from sing-ing?

Text: Robert Lowry, 1860, altered
Music: 87 87, ENDLESS SONG, Quaker Hymn; Robert Lowry, 1860

August Psalm   Psalm 103:1-4,8,10,12-13

Leader: Love your neighbor as yourself…

All: **In this is the supreme law of scripture.**

Side 1 (Leader's side)

Bless the Lord, my soul!
All my inmost being, bless the Holy Name!
Bless the Lord, my soul,
whose benefits are not to be forgotten:

Side 2

Forgiveness of all of your sins,
healing of all your diseases,
crowning you with love and compassion.

1

Compassionate and gracious is the Lord,
slow to anger and abundant in love,
neither treating us in accord with our sins
nor repaying us in accord with our iniquities.

2

As far as the east is from the west
are our transgressions removed.
As a parent has compassion on a child,
so the Lord has compassion on those in awe.

¹
Glory to the Father, and to the Son,
and to the Holy Spirit:

²
As it was in the beginning, is now,
and will be forever. Amen.

Leader: Love your neighbor as yourself...

All: **In this is the supreme law of scripture.**

ORDINARY TIME COMMONS PSALM:

SEPTEMBER

SONG A (Choose one.)

Now thank we all our God
With heart and hands and voi-ces,
Who won-drous things has done,
In whom this world re-joi-ces;
Who from our mo-thers' arms
Has blessed/ us on our way
With count-less gifts of love,
And still is ours to-day.

All praise and thanks to God
Our Ab-ba now be giv-en,
With Son and Spir-it as
They reign in high-est heav-en:
The one e-ter-nal God,
Whom heav-en and earth a-dore!
For thus it was, is now,
And shall be ev-er-more.

Text: see Ecclesiastes 50:22-24; Martin Rinckart, 1636,
translation by Catherine Winkworth, 1858, altered
Music: 67 67 66 66, NUN DANKET; Johann Cruger, 1648

SONG B

Ho-ly, ho-ly, ho-ly, Lord God Al-migh-ty!
　　Ear-ly in the morn-ing
　　　our song shall rise to thee;
　　Ho-ly, ho-ly, ho-ly, mer-ci-ful and migh-ty!
　　God in Three Per-sons, bless-ed Trin-i-ty!

Ho-ly, ho-ly, ho-ly! All the saints a-dore thee,
　　Cast-ing down their gold-en crowns
　　　a-round the glass-y sea;
　　Cher-u-bim and ser-a-phim
　　　fall-ing down be-fore thee,
　　Who was, and is, and ev-er-more shall be.

Ho-ly, ho-ly, ho-ly!
　　Though con-fu-sion hide thee,
　　Glo-ry shin-ing through the blurr
　　　of cloud-ed hu-man view;
　　You a-lone are ho-ly;
　　　there is none be-side thee:
　　Per-fect and pure, your love in all you do.

Ho-ly, ho-ly, ho-ly! Lord God Al-migh-ty!
　　All cre-a-tion praise your name
　　　in earth and sky and sea.
　　Ho-ly, ho-ly, ho-ly, mer-ci-ful and migh-ty!
　　God in Three Per-sons, bless-ed Trin-i-ty!

Text: From Revelation 4:8; by Reginald Heber, 1827, altered
Music: 11 12 12 10, NICAEA; John B. Dykes, 1861

September Canticle   from 1 Peter 2:21-24

Leader: We glory in the Cross…

All: **Of our Lord Jesus Christ, alleluia.**

Side 1 (Leader's side)

To this we are called,
for indeed Christ suffered on our behalf,
leaving us an example to follow in his steps:

Side 2

He did not sin,
nor was guile found in his mouth;
he was reviled and did not revile in return;
suffering, he did not threaten,
but delivered himself to the one judging justly.

1

Our sins he carried in his body
up onto the tree,
that dying to sin, we might live for justice.
By his bruises, we are cured.

2

Glory to the Father, and to the Son,
and to the Holy Spirit:

1

As it was in the beginning, is now,
and will be forever. Amen.

Leader: **We glory in the Cross...**

All: **Of our Lord Jesus Christ, alleluia.**

ORDINARY TIME COMMONS PSALM:

OCTOBER

SONG A (Choose one.)

Ho-ly God\, we praise/ your Name;
Lord of all\, we bow\ be-fore you!
All on earth\ your scep/-ter claim,
All in heav-en a-bove\ a-dore you;
In-fin/-ite\ your vast do/-main,
Ev-er-last\-ing is\ your reign.

Hark! the loud\ cel-es/-tial hymn
An-gel choirs\ a-bove\ are rais-ing,
Cher-u-bim\ and ser/-a-phim,
In un-ceas\-ing chor\-us prais-ing;
Fill the/ heav-ens with sweet ac/-cord:
Ho-ly, ho\-ly, ho\-ly Lord.

Ho-ly Fa\-ther, Ho/-ly Son,
Ho-ly Spir\-it, Three\ we name you;
While in ess\-ence on/-ly One,
Un-div-i\-ded God\ we claim you;
And a/-dor\-ing bend the/ knee,
While we en-ter the mys\-ter-y.

Text: Ignaz Franz, *Grosser Gott,* about 1774,
translated by Clarence Walworth, 1858, altered
Music: 78 78 77 GROSSER GOTT, *Katholisches Gesangbuch, Vienna,* 1774

SONG B

Ho-ly Ma-ry, grace-ful Mo-ther,
Hear your sons and daugh-ters say,
Mo-ther, Bless-ed a-mong wo-men,
For your sons and daugh-ters, pray.

May the grace of Christ our Sa-vior
And the Fa-ther's bound-less love
With the Ho-ly Spir-it's fa-vor
Rest up-on us from a-bove.

Thus may we a-bide in u-nion
With each oth-er and the Lord,
And pos-sess, in sweet com-mu-nion,
Joys which earth can-not af-ford.

Text: Verses 2 & 3 by John Newton, *Olney Hymns*, 1779
Music: 87 87 D, STUTTGART, Christian F. Witt, 1715;
adapted by Henry J. Gauntlett, 1805-1876
Popular melody for: *Come Thou Long Expected Jesus*

October Psalm

Psalm 63:1-8

Leader: I am the Alpha and the Omega:

All: **My kingdom is everlasting, alleluia!**

Side 1 (Leader's side)

God, you are my God; you I earnestly seek.
My soul thirsts for you, my body longs for you,
as in a land with no water, dry and weary.

Side 2

So in the sanctuary I saw you,
beheld you in your power and glory.
Your love is better than life itself;
my lips will glorify you.

1

So I will praise you in all the ways I am alive;
in your name I will lift up my hands.

2

As with fatness and richness,
my soul will be satisfied;
with singing lips my mouth will sing praise.

1

When I remember you on my bed,
through the night watches I think of you,
you who are my help;
then in the shadow of your wings I sing.

2

My very self stays close to you;
your right hand upholds me.

1

Glory to the Father, and to the Son,
and to the Holy Spirit:

2

As it was in the beginning, is now,
and will be forever. Amen.

Leader: I am the Alpha and the Omega:

All: **My kingdom is everlasting, alleluia!**

ORDINARY TIME COMMONS PSALM:

NOVEMBER

(until Advent)

SONG A (Choose one.)

Praise God, from whom all bless-ings flow;
Praise God, all crea-tures here be-low;
Praise God a-bove, ye heav'n-ly host!
Praise Fa-ther, Son, and Ho-ly Ghost.

For maj-es-ty and migh-ty deeds,
With blast of horn and tam-bou-rine,
With harp and dance and flute and string,
Let ev'-ry hu-man breath now sing.

Give praise to reach the migh-ty dome,
Give praise with cym-bals, crash-ing sound,
Give praise with lyre and bless-ed skill,
Praise God to wake the ho-ly hill.

Praise God, from whom all bless-ings flow;
Raise hands, all crea-tures here be-low;
Praise God, our Fa-ther and the Son
And Ho-ly Spir-it, Three in One.

Text: from Psalm 150; vs 1 by Thomas Ken, 1695, altered;
vs 2,3 by Stephen J. Wolf, 2009
Music: OLD HUNDREDTH, LM, Louis Bourgeois,
first published in *Genevan Psalter*, 1551

Je-ru-sa-lem/, my hap-py home\,
When shall I come/ to thee?
When shall my sor/-rows have an end\?
Your joys when shall\ I see?

The saints are crowned/ with glo-ry great\;
They see God face/ to face;
They tri-umph still/, they still re-joice\,
No grief or wor-ry their case.

King Da-vid stands/, his harp in hand\
As lea-der of/ the choir:
Ten thou-sand times/ that we be blessed\,
That we his mu\-sic hear.

Our La-dy sings/ Mag-ni-fi-cat\
With tune sur-pass/-ing sweet,
And all the vir/-gins bear their part\,
While sit-ting at\ her feet.

And Mag-da-len/ has left her grief\,
With cheer-ful joy/ does sing
And bless-ed saints/, their har-mo-ny\
To ev-'ry room\ they bring.

Je-ru-sa-lem/, Je-ru-sa-lem\,
God grant that I/ may see
Your end-less joy/, and of the same\
Par-ta-ker al\-ways be.

Text: F.B.P., London, around 1583, altered
Music: C.M., 86 86, LAND OF REST, traditional American melody

November Canticle   Colossians 1:12-20

Leader: The Church's true foundation…

All: **Is Jesus Christ the Lord, alleluia.**

Side 1 (Leader's side)

Give joyful thanks to the Father
who made you fit
for your part of the lot of the saints in light,

Side 2

Who delivered us out of the authority of night
and transitioned us into the kingdom
of the beloved Son in whom we are redeemed
in the forgiveness of our sins.

1

The Son is the image of the invisible God,
the firstborn of all creation.
In him all things were created,
in the heavens and on the earth,
the visible and the invisible,
even thrones, lordships, rulers and authorities.

2

All things have been created
through him and for him.
He is before all things,
and in him all things hold together.

1

He is the head of the body, the Church,
and the beginning, the firstborn from the dead,
that in all things he may hold the first place.

2

In him all fullness was well pleased to dwell,
and through him reconciliation to himself
    of all things,
things on earth and things in the heavens,
making peace through the blood of his cross.

1

Glory to the Father, and to the Son,
and to the Holy Spirit:

2

As it was in the beginning, is now,
and will be forever. Amen.

Leader: The Church's true foundation

All: **Is Jesus Christ the Lord, alleluia.**

ORDINARY TIME COMMONS PSALM:

Apostles	Sundays	page 88
Martyrs	Mondays	page 90
Holy Women	Tuesdays	page 92
Pastors & Doctors	Wednesdays	page 94
Holy Men	Thursdays	page 96
Virgins	Fridays	page 98
Mary	Saturdays	page 100

Commons Psalm for
Apostles & Ordinary Time Sundays

Leader: Lord, give us wisdom to seek your face;
open the eyes and ears of our heart, and
help us to see and hear as you desire.

Calling many to follow him,
Jesus chose twelve and made them apostles.
Mk 3:13-19

Praise the Lord, all you nations;
extol the Lord, all you peoples.
Ps 117:1

Great is this steadfast love toward us,
the fidelity of the Lord to forever.
Ps 117:2

The Lord did greatness for us;
we were full of joy.
Ps 126:3

Restore our good fortune, Lord,
like streams in the dry desert.
Ps 126:4

He came and went among us,
and comes and goes in our midst,
to call us as witnesses to the resurrection.
Acts 1:21,22

Going out, the sower goes out weeping,
carrying seeds for the sowing.
Ps 126:6a

Returning, the sower will return
carrying sheaves with a song of joy.
Ps 126:6b

I now call you friends;
hear what I have heard from my Father.
Jn 15:15

You are no longer strangers and aliens,
but equal citizens with the saints
and members of the family of God.
Eph 2:19

You are built on the foundation
of the apostles and prophets,
with Christ Jesus himself as the cornerstone.
Eph 2:20

In Christ the whole building fits together
and grows into a holy temple in the Lord.
Eph 2:21

You also are being built together
into a dwelling place of God in the spirit.
Eph 2:22

Glory to the Father and to the Son
and to the Holy Spirit:

As it was in the beginning, is now,
and will be forever. Amen.

SCRIPTURE AND/OR THE "OUR FATHER"

CLOSING PRAISES, page 102

Commons Psalm for
Martyrs & Ordinary Time Mondays

Leader:
Lord, give us courage
to say yes to our vocations
and free us from all fear
except reverence for you.

Whoever declares their very self for me,
I will declare my very self for them.
see Mt 10:32

Give thanks to the Lord who is good,
whose love is to forever.
Ps 118:1

The Lord is with me, I will not be afraid.
What can any human being do to me?
Ps 118:6

I keep this in mind:
the Lord is with me, ready to help me.
Ps 118:7

Better to take refuge in the Lord
than to trust in the human.
Ps 118:8

Who will separate us
from the love of Christ?
Affliction? Distress? Persecution? Famine?
Nakedness? Peril? The Sword?
Rom 8:35

But in all these things we overconquer
through the one who has loved us.
Rom 8:37

I am persuaded that not death, nor life,
nor angels, nor rulers, nor present things,
nor things coming, nor powers,
nor height, nor depth,
Rom 8:38,39a

Nor any other creature will be able
to separate us from the love of God
in Christ Jesus our Lord.
Rom 8:39b

The Lord became my strength and my song
and became to me salvation.
Ps 118:14

Blessed are those who suffer persecution
for the sake of justice;
the kingdom of heaven is theirs.
Mt 5:10

Glory to the Father and to the Son
and to the Holy Spirit:

As it was in the beginning, is now,
and will be forever. Amen.

SCRIPTURE AND/OR THE "OUR FATHER"

CLOSING PRAISES, page 102

Commons Psalm for
Holy Women & Ordinary Time Tuesdays

Leader:　　Lord, give us right judgment
　　　　　to discern your call in freedom
　　　　　and make us wise
　　　　　in the ways you wish us to be wise.

Make it in Israel a statute
to praise the name of the Lord.
Ps 122:4b

For the sake of my sisters
and brothers and friends
I will say, "Now, peace be within you."
Ps 122:8

For the sake of the house of the Lord our God
I will seek your prosperity.
Ps 122:9

Deep calls to deep in roaring waterfalls.
All your waves and breakers sweep over me.
Ps 42:8

Put hope in God, whom I will yet praise,
my saving help and God.
Ps 42:12b

I am your servant, born of your handmaid,
a feeble human with a short life
and a weak understanding of justice and laws.
Wis 9:5

With you is Wisdom, who knows your works
and was present when you created the world.

Wis 9:9a

She knows what is pleasing in your eyes
and right in accord with your ordinances.

Wis 9:9b

She knows and understands all things
and will guide me to prudence in my actions
and guard me in her magnificence.

Wis 9:11

Give me Wisdom,
your companion at your throne.

Wis 9:4a

Send her forth from the holy heavens
and dispatch her from your majestic throne.

Wis 9:10a

May she labor beside me
and so may I learn what pleases you.

Wis 9:10b

Glory to the Father and to the Son
and to the Holy Spirit:

As it was in the beginning, is now,
and will be forever. Amen.

SCRIPTURE AND/OR THE "OUR FATHER"

CLOSING PRAISES, page 102

Commons Psalm for Pastors & Doctors
& Ordinary Time Wednesdays

Leader: Lord, give us knowledge
of what Jesus teaches
known in the triumph of your mercy
over judgment, even justice.

You are the light of the world;
a city set on a hill cannot be hidden.
Mt 5:14

Give praise sun and moon;
give praise all stars shining.
Ps 148:3

Give praise, you heavens of the heavens
and waters above the skies.
Ps 148:4

From the rising of the sun to its setting
praised be the name of the Lord.
Ps 113:3

Hallelujah! Praise the Lord, my soul!
I will sing praise to my God while I still am.
Ps 146:1,2

Put your trust not in princes
nor humans in whom there is no salvation.
Ps 146:3

Their spirits depart, they return to the ground,
and that day their plans come to nothing.
Ps 146:4

The one staying faithful to forever
defends the cause of the oppressed
and gives food to the hungry.
Ps 146:6b,7a

The Lord sets prisoners free
and gives sight to the blind.
Ps 146:7b,8a

The Lord watches over alien strangers
and sustains the orphan and the widow.
Ps 146:9ab

What I have learned about wisdom,
this I freely share, without hiding her riches.
Wis 7:13

She is an inexhaustible treasure;
those who gain her are friends with God.
Wis 7:14

The one who does the commandments
and teaches them
will be called great in the kingdom of heaven.
Mt 5:19b

Glory to the Father and to the Son
and to the Holy Spirit:

As it was in the beginning, is now,
and will be forever. Amen.

SCRIPTURE AND/OR THE "OUR FATHER"

CLOSING PRAISES, page 102

Commons Psalm for
Holy Men & Ordinary Time Thursdays

Leader:
Lord, give us reverence
for the ways of the Father
through the holiness
that comes only from you.

The Lord reigns, robed in majesty;
robed is the Lord and armed with strength.
Ps 93:1a

More than thunders of great waters
or mighty breakers of the sea,
mighty in the height is the Lord.
Ps 93:4

Bless the Lord, all you works of the Lord,
exalt and sing praise to forever.
Dan 3:57

You waters above the heavens,
bless the Lord,
all you powers, bless the Lord.
Dan 3:60,61

Sun and moon, bless the Lord,
stars of heaven, bless the Lord.
Dan 3:62,63

You fire and heat, bless the Lord,
you ice and cold, bless the Lord.
Dan 3:66,69

You nights and days, bless the Lord,
you light and darkness, bless the Lord.
Dan 3:71,72

Let the earth bless the Lord;
exalt and sing praise to forever.
Dan 3:74

You seas and rivers, bless the Lord,
you springs and rain, bless the Lord.
Dan 3:78,77

Give thanks to the Lord, who is good,
whose mercy endures to forever.
Dan 3:89

Bless the God of "*gods*,"
all you who worship the Lord.
Dan 3:90a

Sing praise and give thanks
to the One God
whose mercy endures to forever.
Dan 3:90b

Glory to the Father and to the Son
and to the Holy Spirit:

As it was in the beginning, is now,
and will be forever. Amen.

SCRIPTURE AND/OR THE "OUR FATHER"

CLOSING PRAISES, page 102

Commons Psalm for
Virgins & Ordinary Time Fridays

Leader: Lord, give us understanding
of our baptism in Christ
and set fire in us your confirming love.

God strengthens the bars of your gates
and blesses your peoples within you,
Ps 147:13

Grants peace to your border,
and satisfies you with finest of wheat.
Ps 147:14

Blessed are the pure of heart,
for they shall see God.
Mt 5:8

If the Lord does not build the house,
the builders labor in vanity.
Ps 127:1a

If the Lord does not watch over the city,
the watcher stands guard in vain.
Ps 127:1b

It is vanity to rise early or stay up late,
or to eat the bread of hard toil;
Ps 127:2a

The Lord provides
as the beloved get their sleep.
Ps 127:2b

Deep waters cannot quench the love,
and even rivers cannot wash her away.
Song 8:7

If one gave all the wealth of the house
for love,
that one would be scorned and mocked.
Song 8:7

Blessed are the clean of heart,
for they shall see God.
Mt 5:8

Glory to the Father and to the Son
and to the Holy Spirit:

As it was in the beginning, is now,
and will be forever. Amen.

SCRIPTURE AND/OR THE "OUR FATHER"

CLOSING PRAISES, page 102

Commons Psalm for
Mary & Ordinary Time Saturdays

Leader:
Lord, give wonder and awe
in your presence,
and humble clarity to trust
what you want us to ponder.

In the beginning was the Word,
and the Word was with God
and the Word was God.
Jn 1:1

May God be gracious to us and bless us,
may God's face shine upon us.
Ps 67:2

May the peoples praise you, God,
may the peoples praise you, all of them.
Ps 67:4

The land will yield her harvest,
God will bless us.
Ps 67:7

When the fullness of time had come,
God sent forth God's own Son,
becoming of a woman and under the law.
Gal 4:4

That he might redeem those under the law,
that we might receive full adoption
as sons and daughters.
Gal 4:5

All the ends of the earth
will revere our God.

Ps 67:8

They will beat their swords into plowshares
and their spears into pruning hooks.

Is 2:4b

Nations will not take up the sword
and they will train for war no more.

Is 2:4c

House of Jacob, come!
Let us walk in the light of the Lord.

Is 2:5

The Lord has looked with favor
on the servant of the Lord;
the Almighty has done great things for me.

Lk 1:48a,49a

Hail Mary, full of grace,
the Lord is with you;
blessed are you among women and
blessed is the fruit of your womb, Jesus.

Lk 1:28,42

Holy Mary, mother of God,
pray for us sinners,
now and at the hour of our death. Amen.

Lk 1:31,32

SCRIPTURE AND/OR THE "OUR FATHER"

CLOSING PRAISES, page 102

Closing Praises

Saint Francis Psalm of Praise for All Hours

Leader: Praise the Lord forever.

All: **Praise the Lord forever.**

Side 1: Holy, holy, holy   Rev 4:8
is the Lord God Almighty,
who was, who is, and who is to come:

All: **Praise the Lord forever.**

Side 2: Worthy are you,   Rev 4:11
our Lord and our God, to receive
the glory and honor and power:

All: **Praise the Lord forever.**

Side 1: Worthy is the Lamb who was slain
to receive the power and riches
and wisdom and blessing: Rev 5:12

All: **Praise the Lord forever.**

Side 2: Let us bless the Father and the Son
and the Holy Spirit:

All: **Praise the Lord forever.**

Side 1: Bless the Lord,   Dan 3:57
all you works of the Lord:

All: **Praise the Lord forever.**

Side 2: **A**ll you servants of the Lord, Rev. 19.5
praise our God, you small and you great,
who revere God in awe:

All: **Praise the Lord forever.**

Side 1: Let heaven and earth give praise: Ps 69:35a

All: **Praise the Lord forever**

Side 2: And every creature in heaven Ps 69:35b
and on earth and under the earth
with the seas and all moving in them:

All: **Praise the Lord forever.**

Leader: *Glory to the Father and to the Son
and to the Holy Spirit:*

All: **As it was in the beginning, is now,
and will be forever. Amen.**

PRAYER OF SAINT FRANCIS

All: **Almighty, most holy,
you who alone are totally good,
may we give back to you
all praise, all glory, all grace, all honor,
all blessing, and all good.
So be it. So be it. Amen.**

+

CPSIA information can be obtained at www.ICGtesting.com
Printed in the USA
LVOW10s0712180913

352812LV00001B/2/P

9 781937 081027